Around Town

MEET THE MAYOR

By Joyce Jeffries

Gareth Stevens
Publishing

Please visit our website, www.garethstevens.com. For a free color catalog of all our high-quality books, call toll free 1-800-542-2595 or fax 1-877-542-2596.

Library of Congress Cataloging-in-Publication Data

Jeffries, Joyce.
Meet the mayor / by Joyce Jeffries.
  p. cm. — (People around town)
Includes index.
ISBN 978-1-4339-9378-7 (pbk.)
ISBN 978-1-4339-9379-4 (6-pack)
ISBN 978-1-4339-9377-0 (library binding)
1. Mayors—Juvenile literature. 2. Occupations—Juvenile literature. I. Jeffries, Joyce. II. Title.
JS141.J44 2013
352.23'216—dc23

First Edition

Published in 2014 by
Gareth Stevens Publishing
111 East 14th Street, Suite 349
New York, NY 10003

Copyright © 2014 Gareth Stevens Publishing

Editor: Ryan Nagelhout
Designer: Nicholas Domiano

Photo credits: Cover, pp. 1, 5 Photos.com/Thinkstock.com; pp. 7, 19 iStockphoto/Thinkstock.com; pp. 9, 24 (city hall) Hemera/Thinkstock.com; p. 11 Creatas/Thinkstock.com; p. 13 Janne Hamalainen/Shutterstock.com; p. 15 ben bryant/Shutterstock.com; p. 17 Andersen Ross/Blend Images/Getty Images; pp. 21, 23, 24 (speech) Digital Vision/Thinkstock.com; p. 24 (money) Africa Studio/Shutterstock.com.

Printed in the United States of America

CPSIA compliance information: Batch #CS13GS: For further information contact Gareth Stevens, New York, New York at 1-800-542-2595.

Contents

Mayors run towns!

They are part
of the government.

They work at city hall.

People vote them into office.

REGISTER HERE 11

They help fix problems
in town.

13

They help make rules.
These are called laws.

20
M.P.H.

W13-1 DEPT OF TRANSPORTATION

NO PARKING ANY TIM

STOP

Laws keep us safe!

They pick how a town
uses its money.

They speak for the city.

They talk to people
about the city.
This is called a speech.

Words to Know

city hall

money

speech

Index

24